MINING OF A DIAMOND

A BIOGRAPHY-PART 1

BARIRA SIDDIQUI

Made with ♥ on the Notion Press Platform
www.notionpress.com

This book is dedicated to the love of my life- **<u>My Father</u>**

Contents

Preface

Barira Siddiqui is a Teacher, Nutritionist and a Professional Makeup Artist by profession. Her ideal is her father whom she looks up-to each day and gains motivation and courage, He has helped her to be a great person in and out and had given the best mottos in life to seek. She had listened to these stories mentioned in the book since a kid and always had dreamt of telling the world that like her she wants everyone to know her father is a real life superhero.

Barira Siddiqui

New Delhi, India

Mail: barirasiddiquii16@gmail.com

Acknowledgements

KULSUM SIDDIQUI

NAHID SIDDIQUI

NASEEM KHAN

SABIR KHAN

RIYAZ

Prologue

This book is based on real life events. And the past incidents that took place in the life of author's father's life. The book contains all relations and events from the exact moment it happened, there are different timelines and flashbacks involved so you will get into that while reading.

Also all characters are real and the timelines are somewhere not in correct order but will help you understand the storyline better.

CHAPTER ONE

1969:BOMBAY

In year 1969 a boy was born in the city of dreams "Bombay"

Unlike others he bought dreams with him such dreams which every boy in Mumbai dreams of...

His mother named him after the dreams "Mohd. Jahangir Siddiqui".

Like the name his dreams and wishes were royal but the situations and reality was a lot different.

The upcoming struggles in his life which he didn't had any idea about.

PAPA WITH SIBLINGS

CHAPTER TWO

1972: SHEIKH MISRI

They used to live in sheikh misri in a hut made by them, A small area covered with tin sheets, dry grass and sand it was a Kucha house, with everything in one Place altogether without any restroom, to use the washroom they used to go in an open place at Night with the bucket to get fresh.

Dada used to work in film industry as a junior artist, he worked in some amazing classics "Aadmi Sadak Ka", Ek Mahal Ho Sapno Ka" & many more. Dadi used to teach in "Talib-E-Balgha" as an Islamic teacher, both of them wanted to give higher studies to their kids.

At the age of 9, there's this incident that took place- at night a fire accidently started in one of the huts and slowly all the huts nearby started catching that fire and dad's hut also caught fire, eventually my Dadi got aware in time and she woke everyone up my badi phupho, papa and choti phupho. She took the essentials as fast as she can. There was a canal right beside the huts due to the fire and nowhere to go only the way through the canal was left, due to the smoke caused by the fire and the chaos she took everyone and from the way through the canal they crossed it by swimming till the end.

After the fire stopped, they all sat near the burned huts and my dada came back from work he saw everything and asked my Dadi "Kya film ki shooting chalri hai?" and she told him what all happened. They were tensed as they lost the one place they had now with the kids and the things saved from fire where will they go in the middle of the night.

Then Dadi thought of one the aunts and she went to her house it was nearby so they went over to their house and stayed for 2 nights

In this duration Dadi found a room on rent and they shifted there. And continued the school and work in sheikh misri itself.

The normal routine started again.

One of the days, my dadi went to a house to teach like the other normal days, and there she told the lady about the struggle of living

on rent as the owner asks every now and then to leave and usually asks for more money and advance, she asked the lady if there's any

House or room for rent, there was this lady's brother sitting nearby he heard the whole thing and told dadi about the one house he had

And he lost it due to the demolishing of the building and taken over by the government, he said he got a house in chawl in exchange

But that is taken over by the government and only by finding the file and visiting the office regularly and on some terms & conditions,

But he don't have time for that, so he told dadi that if she wants she can visit the govt. office and get that house and have to pay

50-rupee rent, he will not ask them to leave until they want to.

She agreed and from the next day she started visiting government office every day and used to spend whole day to get through the terms,

She struggled every single day by visiting regularly for the file get passed, and after 1 month the file passed and the

Government official told her that it's officially theirs now.

She went directly to the person who was the actual house owner, he couldn't believe it that she claimed the house on her own from such officials.

He told her that they can start living there and from the next day they all shifted there, and started living in the chawl in Bandra.

CHAPTER THREE

1976:AMROHA

Badi phupho ki shaddi fix hui unke phupho ke bete se

Or sab log bombay se amroha aye, functions hue or ghar ghar mai shaddi hui...

Ye wo waqt tha jaha papa first time naseem taya se miley or dadi ne unhe introduce karaya unse ye keheke ke tumhare mama ka ladka hai ye, us waqt pe ye sab ladkey bheneo ki shaddi mai kaam karane ke wajah se bohot mashuur theey.

Aur wahi se naseem taya ne bohot help karai phupho ki shaddi mai wo time esa tha ke bina ek second ruke jo barish shuru hui ti toh puri shaddi itni zyada tez barish thi ke kaam ruke nahi uske wajah se naseem and friends ne bohot help kiya tha. Wahi se papa and unka bond banna shuru hua or unka bond friendship mai badal gaya..

CHAPTER FOUR

1980:BANDRA

The first reaction to such house of their own as it was a pakka house with cement walls, and a little area in front for kitchen.

Since the next day dada started bringing one utensil per day because they didn't own any household kitchen items.

The one thing they got happy about was for the whole chawl they had one washroom near the first house of the chawl.

A mellow afternoon and the wind banging in the doors a small chawl somewhere in Bombay in,

He came home after his school to his mother making teddy bears and his sister doing house hold chores,

Seeking for food and all of them getting ready for lunch and eating in a single plate to survive the

Day as they remember the times when they didn't even had this single plate food and used visit relatives

House so that they could offer some lunch but the relatives usually ignored them. Coming from those flashbacks

They started thanking god for a single plate food and had that for the day. He stood up and went towards the door to go out to play as he reached the door, he passed through his father who was drenched in sweat as he was coming back,

From repairing a lift in this scorching heat, standing there that moment itself he passed a realization of observing the

Present stage of life and seeking for a change and a better life. Since that moment it jabbed inside him and he started working on it to make a better future not only for himself but for his family, selflessly he started studying in the day

And worked in the afternoon till night. Even after having a strict family background that didn't kept him from working for

His dreams. He started coming home late from work and his dad used to lock the house so he couldn't enter, his big sister were

Always awake after everyone slept he helped him sneak in and served the leftover food to him in the morning the same day repeats.

He started working by collecting scrap and making it into envelope, some days went by and he saved enough to work

More than this he started selling toys by the road in traffic signals and saving all at the end he handed over to his mother.

Days went by and this grind didn't stop balancing work and studies was hard but that's what he signed up for a dream that

Every boy from chawl sees and not every one of them achieve. The days were hard the night were tough, the struggle was real

But watching his mother and father worked for their survival, he realized he had to put them off the burden they are carrying. All day every day he started working and when the days he handed his saving to his mother and his mother's prayers

Worked as magic for him, he started excelling in studies and passed through his school, while balancing his work alongside.

He has always been a cricket lover, One day he was being stubborn about going in a match tournament but dadi dada was not allowing him to, but still he started wearing shoes and said he will go. Dada got angry started walking towards him with a stick, phupho tried to stop him but he didn't stop, he was about to beat him with the stick but dad run away from there to the grounds.

That evening dada dadi told phupho to lock door and to not give him dinner, everyone went to sleep and once dad came home

Around 12:00 a.m., He opened the lock by help of a comb he used to carry, dada dadi used to sleep in the entrance area where the kitchen was, slowly and quietly he sneaked in and badi phupho sneaked in the kitchen area and quietly served the dinner to him after that they went to sleep.

Next day when dada-dadi asked when did he came back home, phupho used to cover up saying he came early at 9.

Years gone by, He passed his class and completed his school

CHAPTER FIVE

1981-1988

He applied for the engineering, it was a night college he used to study there from 7 p.m. till 10 p.m. at night.

After coming back from college and having dinner he used to study, later getting some rest. In the early morning he woke up and went with his father (my dadaji) he got the job there to assist him in repairing the lift in some weeks from assistance he started working on his own as an independent lift repairmen. He started working there full day and in the evening from the day off from work, coming back to home changing and going all the way to for studies and studying overnight with dedication and hard work he completed his degree.

But because of some corrupted disappointments in our education system. The result was not being released without being bribed, the professors asked everyone to bring money if they need their degrees, that time dada nor dadi could afford the amount they were asking, so all the hard work and those years felt like wasted to him, dadi saw papa's state and his dreams being chained up by those corrupted idiots, she decided to arrange it anyhow and she was successful in bringing back dad's smile both dada dadi had a word and they paid the amount and got his degree.

After getting the degree he was looking up for opportunities but was not getting the desired place to work.

And continued to work as a repairmen in lift. When he got his first salary he gave it to dadi it was 900/ rupees, dadi asked him what he wanted to buy he asked for new shoes, dadi took him to market and bought him a 700 rupee shoes that time without giving any thought of saving or anything it was his first salary.

CHAPTER SIX

1989:BOMBAY/ DELHI

Delhi 1989:

Choti phupho ki shaddi fix hui,

Foziya appo ki shaddi rehan phupha se fix hui wo bombay se malviya nagar settle hue shaddi k baad

Or waha se sab shaddi ke functions khatam hone ke baad wapis sab ghar wale bombay aye.

• KALYAN, BOMBAY: 1989

After some months,

Dadi visited her big brother in kalyan and told him about my father and asked for some work if there's any type of position where papa could work for part time. And this time he got the job in TATA Company and he continued to work in this company for 2 year with dedication till he got promoted and was offered the job in TATA's Dubai Company.

CHAPTER SEVEN

1992:DUBAI

He accepted the offer and went to Dubai, leaving his family and loved ones which was very difficult for him. Continued to work there for a year and used to call from a PCO to talk with his family back in India.

One day when he was calling from a PCO the call wasn't able to connect due to network issue after trying for 2-3 times, he asked the person behind him to take his turn and stood beside the telephone booth, while the person was trying the number his call was also unable to connect papa saw that person trying to call on an Indian number, he then asked him if he was from India as well papa thought his face was similar and that he saw him somewhere but wasn't able to recognize the face,

After his call trials he asked papa to try once and this time call got connected, after having the conversation with loved ones, he came back to his place and turned on the TV. Well that phone booth person was none other than shahrukh khan. (Like whaaattttt??......I know papa sochenge ye kyu dala biography mai, but I couldn't stop myself from adding this part...)

DUBAI: DIVING & WATERSPORT CENTRE

CHAPTER EIGHT

BONUS:RIYAZ UNCLE'S STORY

[RIYAZ UNCLE'S STORY SIDE OF HOW-HE MET MY DAD]

We had just finished Power Transformer Oil filtration and were about to leave Malad substation, my colleague Nadeem S Janaki insisted to wait as he was expecting his bike from someone known to be Jahangir.

A handsome guy bit nervous in his appearance entered the premises with a bleeding ear on scooter. I recall he got brushed while his scooter skid on the road. This was the first I was introduced to Jahangir Siddiqui. As we were parting Nadeem asked him to continue with the ride to instill confidence.

Further on, we used to meet regularly at work and it continued for a while getting introduced to several personalities with inhibited Bombaya styles. I was asked to get ready for deputation for Dubai Project in this routine we rarely met and forgot each other for a while. After a lapse of 4months of my joining Dubai project I was told by one of my Colleague Anik Kuwari that Jahangir Siddiqui, the black Salman Khan is expected to join Dubai project in couple of days. We were allocated different blocks for stay in Satwa area of Bur Dubai. During off hours we occasionally used at residences and interact regularly as I was in supervisor charge for the Central Control room & Jahangir was an expert for the Maxitermi termination works.

Days passed there were highs and lows in the project with respect interaction of personalities and growing groupism surfaced in the working group of TEC at Dubai.

Project execution pressure were evident with the passage of time meantime with the outcome of an accident one of our colleague Mr. Anik Kuwari was force to leave the project. This was the time a fresh low in atmosphere and insecurity was felt.

One fine day Jahangir came to me and insisted that I should not decline for the requested help, to first I thought he was joking as we use to have lot of fun together. He narrated that he had come across a girl who was desperately trying to reach her parents and upon enquiry it was revealed that the girl had come to Dubai with a hope of getting a job in beauty Salon which ended up in a nightmare.

I tried to convince Jahangir that this is not in our capacity to get her relieved and big shots will be involved. Jahangir was bent upon to speak to her and her employers to get her off noting that he had contacted back home, her father had collapsed upon hearing her fate and her mother was in a depressed state.

Upon meeting the Employer's representative in Al Musalla Towers in Bur Dubai we were told to pay the certain amount as dues, by her employer and get here relieved. Somehow we managed to get her relieved but this news reached to our office and snow balled into a controversy. This made Jahangir more desperate and somehow he wanted to go back to India out of this fold. We often used to go Cornice at Bur Dubai and discuss things at personnel level, one day Jahangir spilled out his past where he had to overcome much of hardships which made me feel to the extreme. I insisted Jahangir to continue in Dubai till the financial wellbeing back home is improved his desperation to return back continued. I kept the things to myself praying in Allah that someday I will be of some help to him. It was during this time vacancies appeared in DEWA and the polarization within our group was at peak. Jahangir was desperate to return back to Bombay, not willing to continue.

One day I got the application form from DEWA and forced Jahangir to sign the blank form and attend pre-interview session with one of my relative to get familiar for the formal interview. Jahangir faced the interview Al Hamdolillah he got selected. He was in no bound, it was one of the happiest day I could feel for myself.

We parted our ways as Jahangir had to join DEWA & I had to quit TATA's to join private company in Dubai. For the Visa change I had to transit the country and had to see my parents as well. On the way back from Bombay I met Jahangir's mother, this was the first time I met Jahangir's mother at Bandra. I could not imagine her feelings. I recall the sweets offered by Jahangir's mother on return at Bombay Airport were ripped off by Customs intrigued by the Bombay blasts.

After a year or so of my return it was Jahangir's turn planning for his wedding day after having continued for 2 years in DEWA. Having enjoyed the wedding with all his friends he was in no mood to continue in DEWA, this time embroiled with his partner's affection. It was this time that

Jahangir opted for a new home in Okhla. And we met at Bur Dubai Cornice this time he told one of the wishes is fulfilled.

After 1 year it was time to call his partner on a visit Visa to Dubai after long struggle due to the restrictions for Family Visit Visa. It was during the last days of stay of Jahangir's spouse, Jahangir had taken the final call to return back. After a month of return of Jahangir's wife, Jahangir called me and said that he will be leaving once for all.

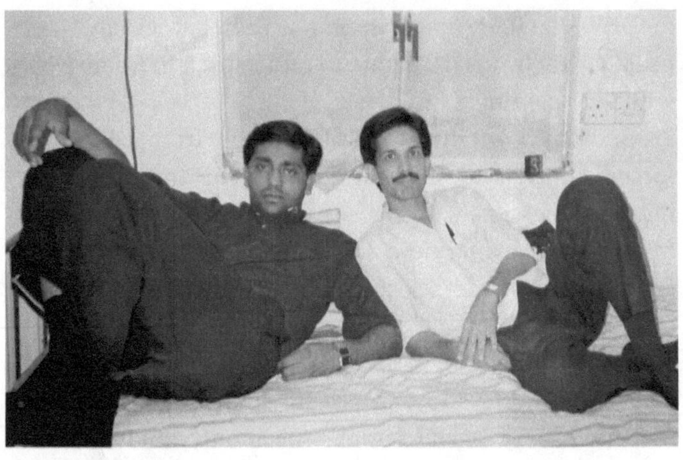

RIYAZ UNCLE(RIGHT) WITH PAPA

Years passed we met again in Delhi in 2002 with his kids, Al Hamdolillah he was well off after period of almost 2 years of hardship.

CHAPTER NINE

1992:AMROHA

Dadi came to amroha to ask badi phupho about the girl whose proposal was put on hold because dadi wanted to confirm from both the phupho about the girl. She came to amroha to meet badi phupho in her sasural and phupho refused to the girl,

She said "Bombay Ki ladki mat dekho, amroha Ki dekho warna yaha se bhi connection khatam hojayega, ek hi toh Bhai hai".

Then next day dadi asked phupho if she wants to go back to Bombay with her. They packed the stuff and dadi called Rauf uncle (Bombay) to book tickets he said he has arranged them and dadi has to go to one of rauf uncle's relative in a mohalla in amroha, dadi got the address and in the evening she went to the address and it was of kaser nani (one of my nani).

There she met kauser khalu (my nani's first son in law) while seated and waiting for the tickets there she saw a lady sitting near, And they greeted each other, she was my nani they had a little conversation my nani asked her why she came all the way here from Bombay, dadi replied "mera mayka hai yaha, meri beti ki shaddi yahi hui hai, ussi se milne ayi thi. Aur app?" .Nani said "mere behen ka ghar hai ye, Milne ayi thi meri ladki ka rishta aya hai ussi silsiley mai, abhi pakka nahi hua hai.

Mashwara lene ayi Hu." dad told her "agar ye ladka sahi Na lagey toh mera bhi ek beta hai appki adaat achi lagi mujhe app chaho

Toh usse bhi mil lena". Nani said "app yaha se jate hue Delhi toh aogy, ek baar hamare ghar bhi aana app nizamuddin ake "zaki hotel"kisi se bhi Puchogy wo apko bata dega, ayega zaroor hume acha lagega." they both then greeted and dadi went back to phupho's home. She told her about the scenario and said will visit them while going back to Bombay. Next day they board the train from amroha and reached Delhi.

CHAPTER TEN

1992:DELHI

they reached Delhi, dadi told her that let's visit the lady's house we met in amroha she insisted so much, so they went over to nizamuddin to visit mom's house, there they saw mom braiding her hair into ribbon she was wearing a pink Pakistani dress. She was alone at home and seeing the two unknown ladies asking for nani she said that "ammi pasdos mai gayi hai app baithe mai bulake lati hu" mom ran to call nani from my another nani's house (in general i have 7 nanis and most of them live in the same area, in case you hearing nani word alot), while mom was gone dadi asked phupho "kesi lagi ladki? "phupho boli "kon ladki" dadi ne ishara kiya "wahi jo abhi gayi hai apni ammi ko bulane" phupho boli "ammi, abhi bhai settle nahi hua hai, kaam shuru hua hai or ye log hamare yahan karenge apko lagta hai." dadi ne kaha "adaat bohot achi hai unki or beti bhi wesi hi hogi, baat karne mai kya jata hai wo bhi ladka dekh rahi hai baat aagy badhi toh dekhengy."

Nani side wale ghar mai baithe thi choti nani ke sath unke ghar pe, unhone suna jab wo foran mummy se boli abid mama (who was mom's cousin) unse bolkar aao nashte ka intezam karein jaldi se." Ye sunkar mummy bhaagi unhe bulane ke liye or nani ghar wapis ayi, wo dadi se mili badi phupho se mili aur or fir unmai khoob batein Hui. Dadi ne bola ke unhein Jana hai train hai unki wapsi ki, toh nani ne phupho ke dono beto ko namkeen biscuits and chips pakda diye "ke app yaha nahi khaa paye raste mai khaa lena train mai".

Train mai wapsi ke waqt dadi or phupho mai baatein Hui isi barein mai or wo sochre te ke papa ko kese bateyngy or unhein kese convince karenge. yaha nani ke ghar yahi baat hori ti ke dadi kya bol gayi ke kya wo proposal tha jo unhone diya ya kya matlab tha uss baat ka kyuki dadi indirectly ye bol gayi ke hamare yahan akar ek baar dekhlo pasand aye toh batana hum fir rishta dengy jo kabhi hua nahi idhar ke ladke ke ghar wale direct rishta late hai ese apne ghar bulakar pehle ladki walo se confirm nahi karte ke wo chahte hai ke ye log aye leke ya nahi.

Dadi on the other hand ye baat islye bol gayi ti kyuki unhe laga nahi tha ke nani gharwale ye rishta karenge kyuki uss waqt ke halat kuch or they papa settle nahi te unke pass khud ka ghar nahi tha jo tha wo itna bada nahi tha or mummy ke ghar or mahol se ekdum alag tha. khair kuch din beet gaye or dadi phupho sab rishte ke barein mai bhul gayi koi zikar hua bhi nahi ghar par iss barein mai, or nani roz isi soch mai thi ke wo kya karein kyuki itni dur ki baat thi Delhi se Bombay 1992 mai koi asaan baat thi nahi, or mummy ko apne se itna dur pehle kabhi kiya nahi tha, nani ne ghar par iss barein mai jab baat ki toh nana ne unse kaha "hum nahi kar rahe itnaa dur", shehzad mama (mom's big brother) ne kaha "dekhlo agar ladka or gharwalo ki adaat achi hai toh dur mat dekho, mai plane se ana jana karwa lia karunga, hum ate jate rahengy, pehle ladkey ko dekhlo or fir faisla lo".

Nani ne fir mere chote nana (sabir khan) se baat ki or unhe sab bataya jo bhi baat dadi se hui or fir unse bola ke "tum bombai jate rehte ho toh zara bombai jakar inki enquiry karo ke kya karte hai kese hai kis tarah ke hai", toh nana ne apne ek Bombay wale dost ko enquire karne ko bola, fir nana 2-3 din baad khud Bombay gaye or dost se miley unke dost ne unhe papa ke barein mai bataya, bohot chota friend circle hai, baithna sab bataya, nana agle din Delhi ke liye nikle or Delhi pahuchte hi nani se milne gaye or unko papa ki tasveer di uske sath sath unhe bola "meri mano toh rishte ko haan kehdo,ladka bohot shareef hai, ghar wale bhi bohot seedhe log hai unko kuch nahi chahye siwaye ladki ke.

Dadi February mai Delhi wapis ayi choti phupho ke ghar or waha unse baat karke engagement ka plan kiya or 18 February ko date fix ki dadi or choti phupho ne engagement hone ke 1-2 din tak dadi wahi ruki toh uske baad Bombay ke liye nikle nani ne papa ke liye kapde bhijwaye.

Train reached Bombay the next day;

CHAPTER ELEVEN

1992:A YEAR TO REMEMBER

<u>BOMBAY</u>

Dadi reached Bombay showed everyone the ring and dresses badi phupho and papa everyone was shocked as kisi ko bhi ummid nahi ti ke dadi bina inform karein function kar ayi ti.

Papa ne ring pehenli or fir phupho ne sabke saath Delhi aane ka plan kiya sabhi ko sabse milna tha.

Or faisla bhi itna bada tha ke sawal bohot they or wo tha landline ka zamana

Toh hua bhi yehi ke sabne July mai plan hua.

<u>Delhi</u>

<u>July:</u>

Dadi, phupho or papa sab Delhi aya or Milne ke liye humayun tomb decide hua

Waha nani se baat karke dadi ne Milne ko bola,

Nani ne chote nana (sajid nana) ko mummy ke sath bheja humayun tomb mummy bekhabar iss baat se ke waha unhe papa Milne jab sab ka aamna samna hua toh they both felt shy and unko bola gaya baat karne ko ek dusre se or sawal hai agar koi toh puchlo.

Toh hamare 90's ke hero heroine, separate hokar sabse thoda sa baat karne ke liye gaye

Conversation start karte waqt sabse mushkil time wahi hota hai jaha app dono Pehli baar miley ho or situation esi ho ke zindagi ka faisla ussi mulaqat mai lena ho.

Yehi khayal mummy papa ke mind mai hoga uss waqt or unki mulaqat ke dauraan papa ne baat karne ki shuruwaat ki "iss rishte se koi problem toh nahi? Koi pressure toh nahi kisi ghar wale ka?"

Mummy ki side se wahi jawab aya jo uss waqt kisi bhi ladki ka jawab hota agar samne salman khan jesa ladka khada ho.. "ji nahi mujhe koi problem nahi, meri maa or abbu ne kuch soch samajh ke ye rishta kiya hoga or sabne apko pasand kiya"

Thoda der saath ghumne ke baad.Wo ghar agye apne apne.

Amroha:

Nani ne amroha mai function kiya ek chota sa jismai unhone apne sarey relatives se milwaya, or sabhi ko papa bohot pasand kiya.

Delhi:

Amroha ke function se free hokar sab Delhi wapis aye or station se mama unko pick karke ghar laye waha mummy ke bade mamu ne papa or dadi puri family ki dawat ki.

Barish ki shuruwaat hui or ye log bhigte hue wapis ghar ayee...

Kuch din ke baad, papa Bombay wapis chale Gaye or baki sab gharwale yahi stay back karre te.

December:

Babri masjid ki ladai hui, uss ladai ki wajah se bombay mai or pure india mai bohot hungama hua or kayii young ladko ko police utha ke lockup mai dal rahi thi..

Ussi waqt ke dauraan nani roz sher khan ke ghar phone karti ti or unhe bolkar dadi se khabar leti thi khairiyat ki..

Unhi dino maqi ek police wala jo ki dadi dada ko janta tha ghar bhi aya karta tha, wo aaye or akar dadi ko bola ke jald se jald wo papa ko kahin door bhej de warna unhe bhi ese hi le jayngy jis tarah ka mahol tha

Unhi dino mai papa ko dubai ka offer aya 'tata' ki taraf se or unhone wo accept kiya.

Papa dubai chale gaye.

CHAPTER TWELVE

1993:DUBAI TO BOMBAY

Dubai mai unhone bohot mehnat ki or as a intern jaane ke baad bhi unhone apna naam banaya or bhot mehnat ke baad khub tarakki ki

Ke unhone intern se seedhe job offer hui.

Wahi se unka turning point chalu hua..

After an year,

New job ke liye apply karne unhe bombay ane tha,

Wo wapis aye..

Wo log royal enfield mini bullet bajaj sx enduro pe ghuma karte te uska naam inhone bobby rakha tha kyuki bobby movie mai use hui ti. Wo log kahin bhi jane ke liye isi ka use kiya karte te.

ROYAL ENFIELD BAJAJ SX ENDURO (INTERNET
IMAGE)

CHAPTER THIRTEEN

1994:LIFE HAPPENS

Naseem taya papa ke cousin ke saath saath unke friends group ka hissa bhi theey, unke saath papa ne apne best moments nikale hai life ke, it was not possible ke kuch msti ho or uska hissa ye dono na bane..

Naseem taya ko bandstand dekhne ka bohot mann tha wo rehne wale kalyan ke theey roz office ke baad wo papa or sab dosto se kehte mujhe wo dekhne jana hai or yaha se ye log sab unka Mazak banana ko kehte, wo raat ko tala lag jata hai gate pe wo lock ho jata hai.. naseem taya kehte bhi ke wo seaside hai movie mai gate jesa kuch dikha toh nahi kabhi... par ye log unhe convience karlete or inki baton mai aa jate inko pure ek saal tak ese chalaya or uske next year leke gaye jaha unhe pata chala unke saath prank hua hai...

Ye one of the lakh kissa hai unke moments ka endless ways mai ye pura group prank karta tha

Or wapis apply karke dubai gaye..

Wo phone or letters ke zariye baat karte te dadi se

Fir dadi ne mummy papa ki baat chalu karai or papa phir daddi ke sath sath mummy ko bhi phone karte te.

Papa dubai se wapis chutti leke jab aaye te tab mummy ke liye cordless leke aaye te

Jisse direct baat ho sake saath hi gift mai blue lady leke aye te

Ek ring bhi layee te iske sath sath jispai mummy ke naam ka initial tha 'N'

Wo ring ab mujhe mummy ne gift kardi joki mai hamresha saath rakhti hu,

Ek bohot khubsurat suit bhi laye te.

Inhi letters or phone calls, gifts ke saath saath....

Pura saal nikal gaya or fir saal ke akhir mai aya wo time jo itne saal se intezaar tha...

Nana ki tabyat kharab hui or unhe shahi hospital mai admit kiya, dadi delhi ayi unhe dekhne,

Dadi ne unse puchi "tabyat theek hai apki ?"

nana ne unse kaha "tabyat theek nahi hai, agar iss saal shaddi nahi kari app logo ne toh hum nahi kar payngy app tyaari karo or shaddi kro kyuki hamare tabyat hume saath nahi degi.."

Dadi ne unse kaha " ye kesi baatein karre hai app, nahid ke alawa hum kisi ko bahu soch nahi sakte mai nahid ko hi bahu bana kar laungi, shaddi ki baat karti hu mai wapis bombay jakar ghar par app fikar na karein"

<u>BOMBAY:</u>

Dadi ne bombay jakar sabse baat kari or mummy ko phone kiya,

Unhone unse kaha " tumhare papa ne mujhse ache se baat nahi kari iss baari, wo toh kehre te ke isi saal shaddi kardo, hum abhi tyaar bhi nahi, ghar karna hai pehle wo bhi khudka nahi hai, or Jahangir ki naukri lage waqt hi kitna hua hai abhi hume ek saal chahye tha unse baat karo."

Mummy ne reply diya " mai kya bolu mummy unse, app bado ke bech ki baat hai, mai unse kya keh sakti hu dua hi karengy.."

Fir ye khabar papa tak pahuchi Unhone 1-2 week baad call kiya,

Wo mummy se bole "dekho, ek baat hai kyuki wo mene tumpai chorhi hai baad mai ye baat nahi aye ke mene bataya nahi, abhi 1-2 saal lagengy ghar karne mai, or abhi waqt lagega sab ko samhjao ke waqt de thoda".

Mummy ne jawab dia "acha hai, ghar karlo wo toh 1-2 saal mai hojayega par tab mai nahi milungi meri toh shaddi isi saal kardengy abbu. Fir ghar ka kya fayda?".

Papa ne kaha "theek hai jab tumhe objection nahi hai, toh mai karta hu kuch".

2 and a half month baad ki date rakhi or tyaariyan chalu hui,

Naye saal ki date rakhi gayi...

Shehzaad mama ne sab tyaariyan karai or dhoom dhaam se shaddi ki tyaari hue sab.

Shaddi ka waqt aya

Or shuruwaat hui station pe papa ki entry se

Papa ne milkar nani se kaha "dahej jesi ek chiz mere samne na ajaye.. or meher bhi kum rakhna.. shariyaat mai hisaab kitab kum hai lena dena zyada aya nahi hai "

Nani ne haskar Mazak kiya " toh tum daddhi(beard) bhi rakhlo"...

Sab hasne lage or fir waha se sab dadi ke side wale amroha ke liye nikle

Or waha pahuchkar shakur chacha ki kothi mai ruke..

Wahi pe sabne shaddi ki tyaariyan ki or log ikhatta hue,

Yaha delhi mai mummy ki side wale alag zorr shorr se tyaari karre the..

CHAPTER FOURTEEN

<u>**January-**</u>

1 jan, Shaddi ka din- finally shaddi ka din aya or dada ne sabko strictly subah 5 baje bulwa liya tha amroha se nikalne ke liye bus se, sabhi waha waqt pe agye or nikal gaye yaha mummy ki side sab ussi waqt halla or shorr kakrke thakk kar soye te!

Baraat 8 baje hall pahuch gayi or waha koi bhi nahi,

Jaldi se mama ne ghar par khabar kari or nani ne sabko uthaya or dulhaan ko uthaya tyaar hone mai lage sab ke sab subah subah...

Mummy hall pahuchi 12:30 baje or sab baraati ne khana khaya

"nikah" padha gaya or finally shaddi muqammal hui...

Dulha dulhan khane ke liye table pe pahuchte khana khane lage ussi waqt Mummy ke sarey cousins ne papa ko ghera or fir ekdum se unke joote pe tut pade sab, papa ne bhi zorr lgaya or udhar mummy ke cousins ne waha se unke pair pakad liye or foran hi ilyas mama ne papa ko utha liya chair se or dusre taraf foziya appo ne zorr lagaya or unki saree ka pallu fatt gaya isi ladai mai,papa ko uthate hi joote hath mai agye suraiyaa khala ke, unhone sabke saath milkar bhagna shuru kiya waha se or fir sabne joote chupa diye,

Joota churai ki rasam hoti bohot shandaar hai ye choti si nok jhok end tak yaad rehti hai ajj bhi ghar mai iss baat ka zikr hai.

Khair khane ke baad sab stage ke around ikatta hyue or fir rasam puri ki pese deke joote lene wali, afsos yaha joote do paise lo wala gaana nahi hua warna or zyada romanchak hota.

Ruksati ka waqt aya mummy ko leke car tak gaye sab or waha ek maruti 800 mai unko baithane lage mummy ka ruksati mai rote hue itna bura haal tha kyuki zahir hai ek naya sheher or naye log aur ghar se itna dur asaan toh nahi tha uss waqt mai jaha video call or phone call ke log sapne dekhte the bas.

Gaadi mai baithte hue sehre ki wajah se kuch na dekhne ke reason se baithte hue unke sir par gate bohot zorr se laga,or fir jana bhi amroha tha ruksat hokar toh pure raste wo dard bardasht karna bhi pada mummy itni zyada shy or bohot zyada ghabrai hui ti uss wajah se wo kisi se keh bhi nahi payi iss barein mai.

Amroha pahuchne ke baad shakur uncle ke ghar mai sab theey aur waha ke ek room mai mummy ko leke gaye waha unki baki rasam hui sab surat dikhai karne gaye or salami diya 1 din baad amroha mai pehla walima hua.

<u>Delhi-</u>
akar 7 din baad,

Agra gaye sab mummy papa ke saath nani or dadi ki family...

Ek choti si Picnic trip hui... jo ajj tak yad hai sabko

Waha hotels mai sab saath there or waha khub enjoy kiya.

<u>**15 din baad.....**</u>
bombay mai walima hua, jaha sab ikhatta hue..
walime ke baad

Usmani Saab ki car mai Bombay ghume sab museum, juhu, and sab tourist spots ghume...

----

20 January-

Papa se milne nani-mama ki family ayi Bombay..

Papa ko wapsi Dubai jana tha..unke tickets bhi ho gaye te final or job bhi waha intezar kar rahi thi,

Afsos itne um dino mai unko wapis jana pada par ek achi chiz ke ye kum waqt mai hazaro yaadein wo bhi itni khubsurat.. wo leke wapis gaye.

----

22 January-

Papa Dubai chale gaye... or uske baad dadi ne nani or mama ki family ko puri bombay ki tour di,

Wo har jagah saath ghume or khub sari yaadein banai..

Wo tasveer ajj bhi ekdum clear hai jo mene unki trip ki dekhi,

Mere nana nani or dada dadi bohot ache theey,unke dil paani ki tarah saaf unke irade buland or unke khwab apne bacho ko khush dekhna, jo pura bhi hua..

Kuch mahino tak:

Phone pe ek lambe arse tak papa se baat hoti ti mummy or dadi and family ki.

Papa ke piche mummy ki Pehli eid nani ke ghar mani..unke bina kyuki visa leke bar bare ghar ana asaan nahi tha.

uss bich mummy ke dadi ka inteqal hua or waha sab rehke ayee... uss waqt bhi papa majbur theey ke wo waha nahi aa paye

Fir ek din papa ne call pe mummy ko Dubai ane ke liye pucha...

To Be Continued.....

A Little Note:

Ye book mere liye ek sapna tha, wo sapna jo bilkul asaan nahi tha it took me 2 years to complete this part 1, iss bich mene face kiye wo issues jo mene soche bhi nahi theey, ek choti si trip ke dauraan mere laptop se book ki adhi story bhi chali gayi and it delayed my entire project. Ab on my wedding 24.11.22 this is the token of love i could give him

Par I didn't gave up..i started all over again and here I am with this part-1

Will soon complete my part-2 of this just keep me and my family in your prayers...

Until next time!